American
Entrepreneurship

WIL MARA

Children's Press®
An Imprint of Scholastic Inc.
New York Toronto London Auckland Sydney
Mexico City New Delhi Hong Kong
Danbury, Connecticut

Content Consultant
Rodney Shrader, PhD
Denton Thorne Chair in Entrepreneurship
University of Illinois at Chicago
Chicago, Illinois

Library of Congress Cataloging-in-Publication Data
Mara, Wil.
American entrepreneurship / Wil Mara.
pages cm.—(A true book)
Includes bibliographical references and index.
Audience: Age 9–12
Audience: Grades 4 to 6
ISBN 978-0-531-24775-4 (lib. bdg.) — ISBN 978-0-531-28461-2 (pbk.)
1. Entrepreneurship—United States—Juvenile literature. 2. Business enterprises—United States—Juvenile literature. I. Title.
HB615.M365 2014
338'.040973—dc23   2013004188

All rights reserved. Published in 2014 by Children's Press, an imprint of Scholastic Inc.
Printed in China 62
SCHOLASTIC, CHILDREN'S PRESS, A TRUE BOOK™, and associated logos are trademarks and/or registered trademarks of Scholastic Inc.
1 2 3 4 5 6 7 8 9 10 R 23 22 21 20 19 18 17 16 15 14

Front cover: Business grand opening
Back cover: Carpenter

Find the Truth!

Everything you are about to read is true *except* for one of the sentences on this page.

Which one is **TRUE**?

T or F Warren Buffett made his fortune in the computer industry.

T or F Andrew Carnegie made his fortune in the steel industry.

Find the answers in this book.

3

Contents

THE **BIG** TRUTH!

Major Players

Howard Hughes was a successful entrepreneur in many different fields.

The United States is the world's richest country.

The Business of America

U.S. president Calvin Coolidge once said, "The business of America is business." The United States would not be the world power it is today without encouraging its citizens to achieve such great success in business. Even in the country's earliest days, laws supported people who hoped to launch their own business **ventures**. Many Europeans made the long, dangerous journey across the Atlantic Ocean to make their business dreams realities.

More than 20 million people emigrated to the United States between 1880 and 1920.

Risks and Possibilities

The United States was a brave new world back then. Taking risks on new ideas became a normal part of life. Americans developed industries that would become the envy of other nations. People dared to invent new products. America grew westward, building railroads and factories. Workers took pride in their trade. American business became famous for creativity, drive, and determination. It also became famous for its **entrepreneurs**, the people who started these businesses.

As technologies improved, especially during the 1800s, fabrics and other goods could be made faster and better.

Many American entrepreneurs start as small business owners.

Some entrepreneurs take a hobby they love and turn it into a growing business.

Some of the greatest entrepreneurs of all time made their fortunes on American soil. New ones are showing up all the time. What is most interesting, though, is that these people often seem to share a few characteristics. By studying these habits and traits, you can learn a great deal—and, hopefully, begin to write your own story of success!

A bright idea can be inspired by just about anything.

10

A Land of Vision

Every success story in the history of American business began the same way: someone had an idea. Successful entrepreneurs are often called **visionaries**. They see possibilities that others don't, and they see how to make those possibilities work. They get a feeling inside—some call it **intuition**—about how to turn their vision into reality. Sometimes they can't put these feelings into words, but they still know they're on the right track.

 Some ideas take time. Thomas Edison took one and a half years to make his lightbulb.

Seeing What Isn't There

Inspiration can come from anywhere. Sometimes it is just a matter of noticing what is missing. Perhaps an existing product has uses that no one considered before. Or maybe a completely new invention could make a task easier or even make it possible for the first time. An entrepreneur can often find success by supplying something people never realized they wanted or needed.

An idea might come from seeing how one object could be adapted to serve another purpose—like turning a lawn mower into a snowmobile.

Steve Jobs (right) founded Apple with his friend Steve Wozniak (left).

Steve Jobs was one of the greatest visionaries the United States has ever seen. He started a computer company in the garage of his parents' home back in 1976. He called the company Apple because he and a friend had spent a summer picking apples on a nearby farm. Computers had been around for a while, but they were used almost exclusively by experts and in businesses.

The iPhone, iPad, and iPod have helped make computer technology easier and more fun to use for the average person.

Jobs's vision was for something called a "personal" computer—one that could be used in the home. Some people thought he was crazy, but he believed in his idea. He wanted to make computers more "user friendly" and fun. By the 1980s, Apple was earning millions of dollars a year. In the 2000s, Jobs helped design the iPod, the iPhone, the iPad, and other devices that many people now use every day.

Daring to Be Different

Many people get ahead in business by following the rules and doing what they are told. But the most successful entrepreneurs do things a little differently. To come up with a new idea, one must think about things in a **unique** way. This is often called "thinking outside the box." It means trying something that hasn't been done before. It also means taking an approach that might seem ridiculous at first but can change the world.

Inventor Bryan Rawlings shows off a pair of his Booster Blades, which a person pedals like riding a bicycle to move forward.

15

Origami Owl charms include letters, words, birthstones, and other objects.

In 2010, 14-year-old Isabella Weems knew she wanted a car when she turned 16. To earn the money to buy one, Weems started a business. With some help from her parents, she invested in supplies for a new kind of locket, which she called a Living Locket. Each of Weems's clear lockets was filled with tokens the customer chose. Weems named her business Origami Owl, and she and her mom started selling lockets at events and home jewelry parties.

Origami Owl's personalized lockets quickly gained popularity. Weems wanted to give other women the same opportunities that she'd had to follow their own dreams. With this in mind, Origami Owl started allowing individuals as young as 14 to earn money selling Living Lockets. So many people signed up, the company was forced to put some of them on a waiting list. Today, Origami Owl has thousands of independent designers across the United States.

Customized jewelry has become a popular business.

Talk About Different!

Born in 1905, Howard Hughes became the wealthiest man of his time. He designed airplanes that changed the aviation **industry**, built medical institutes, made movies, and helped develop Las Vegas, Nevada. He also had some strange habits. In his later years, he lived only in hotel rooms and had almost no contact with people. He was so afraid of germs that he only touched things if they were covered in a thick wad of tissues.

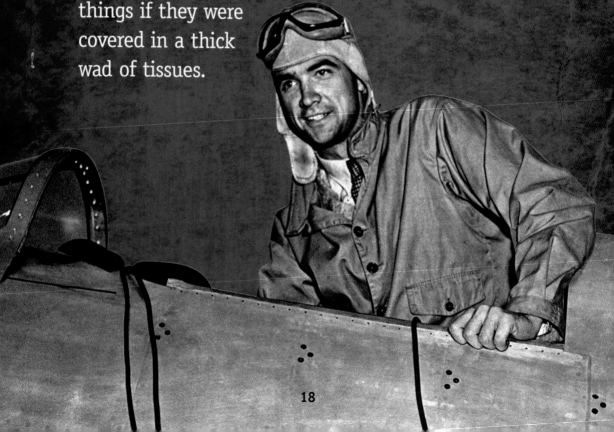

Loving Every Minute of It

American entrepreneurs are often measured by how much money they've made. But many of these same people point out that a big part of their success was getting involved in a business they really cared about. When you love what you do, it helps to carry you through the tough times—and there will *always* be tough times. That's when a person's dedication is pushed to the limit.

When first starting a small business, such as dog walking, it can take time for the business to grow.

Even as a little girl, Kyle Smitley was concerned about the environment. After finishing college, she moved to Washington, D.C., to study environmental law. When she was asked to research the fashion industry, she was alarmed to learn that many clothing **manufacturers** were harming the environment. Inspired, she launched her own line of children's clothes that were truly environmentally friendly. She named her company Barley and Birch, and used only 100 percent organic cotton and water-based dyes.

Clothing manufacturers cause some pollution by importing supplies, such as shipping cloth from factories in China to the United States.

One activity Kyle Smitley helps support is educating farmers in safer and more effective farming methods.

When Smitley tried to sell her new clothing line to **retailers,** she was turned down flat. During this difficult time, her passion kept her going. She got on the Internet and started spreading the word through Web sites. Soon her clothes were so popular among parents that retailers began to call her. Now Barley and Birch is a huge success, and Smitley gives a percentage of her profits to other environmental projects around the world.

When starting a business, do some research—read, ask questions, and try out a few ideas.

CHAPTER 3

The More You Know

There's a very ugly word in the English language: *ignorance*. To be ignorant is to know little or nothing about a topic. No one gets very far by being ignorant. Think of it like taking a test in school—if you don't know anything about the subject, you're going to fail. If you studied hard and learned a lot, you're going to do very well. This rule is the same in business.

 About 84 percent of adults in the world are able to read.

Knowledge Is Power

Andrew Carnegie was born to a poor family that shared a one-room cottage with another family. He got his first job at the age of 13. By the time Carnegie was 18 years old, he was working for a railroad company in Pennsylvania. In his spare time, he got to know all of the most important local businessmen. He also learned how their businesses operated.

Carnegie was born in Scotland. His family moved to the United States when he was a teenager.

Andrew Carnegie was largely self-taught. He educated himself by reading books in his free time.

At his railroad job, Carnegie watched his boss carefully and asked questions. He also read any book he could find. His desire to learn moved him quickly up the company's ranks.

After the Civil War (1861–1865), Carnegie became involved in the iron and steel industries. He continued to ask questions, read, and pay attention to every detail. By the start of the 20th century, he was one of the wealthiest people in the world.

If you don't understand something at school—or anywhere else—ask questions!

All Information Can Be Useful

There are countless examples of American entrepreneurs becoming successful through lessons they'd learned earlier in life. You just never know if something is going to be useful later on. Very few people have become successful with the attitude, "I don't need to learn that—I'm never going to need it." Every experience can lead to something bigger and better.

In college, Mark Zuckerberg designed an interactive Web site called Facemash. People viewing the site chose which of two students' pictures was more attractive. College administrators quickly shut it down because they felt the site was inappropriate. But Zuckerberg remembered Facemash when he later designed Facebook. Users post basic information about themselves such as birthday, hobbies, photos, and so on. Facebook became a global phenomenon, and today has more than one billion users.

Mark Zuckerberg and his company are always working on ways to improve Facebook.

No One Knows It All

The most successful people in American business are not the ones who think they know it all. They're the ones who are willing to admit that they don't. If a person doesn't know something but doesn't admit it, he or she risks making huge mistakes. Every successful entrepreneur has had to learn a thing or two. They set aside their pride and gathered all the information they could find.

A person needs to learn from his or her mistakes to find success in business.

Even after Warren Buffett (right front) invests in a business, he continues learning about the business and the people involved in it.

Warren Buffett is considered the most successful investor in American history. Buffett made his first investment when he was 11 years old. He eventually became the wealthiest person in the world. When he talks about his success, he always says the same thing: if he is interested in a business, he learns as much about it as he can. Buffett spends hours reading reports, talking on the phone, and sometimes traveling to where the business is located.

THE BIG TRUTH!

Major Players

Here's a big truth: the majority of successful entrepreneurs have been men. The business community has often been called a "man's world." But some very savvy women have shattered this tradition and made their own mark on history.

Oprah Winfrey was born into poverty in Mississippi. She went on to become a giant in the media world. She has been a talk show host, producer, actor, and owner of her own network. She also became the first black female billionaire in the world.

Mary Pickford was one of the biggest Hollywood stars of the 1920s. She was a tough and smart negotiator when it came to contracts. Pickford and other actors eventually formed their own studio, called United Artists. It was unusual for any actor to have this much power at the time, especially a woman.

Mary Kay Ash was working at a company that kept promoting men instead of her, even though she worked very hard. Undaunted, she started her own line of cosmetics in 1963. By the 1970s, she was making millions. Ash was committed to making her company a place where people were treated fairly and equally.

Rachael Ray broke into the business world with a book on making meals in less than 30 minutes. She was then invited to appear on television, and soon she had her own show. She has since written several more books, launched her own magazine, and hosted a talk show.

Anyone who opens a business needs to understand that some risk is involved.

CHAPTER **4**

Taking Chances

You may have heard the saying, "The bigger the risk, the bigger the reward." Some of the most successful entrepreneurs got ahead because they were willing to take a chance. Whenever a person has a new idea, there will be others ready to say the idea is crazy. But risk is a normal part of business. If people could make a fortune by playing it safe, everyone would already be rich.

When Cable News Network (CNN) first aired, many people thought it would fail. Some called it the Chicken Noodle Network.

The Big Idea

John Goscha took the first step toward becoming an entrepreneur while still in his teens. In college, he and his friends would hang sheets of paper on the walls of their dorm rooms. They could then use the paper to write down their ideas. But tearing down old sheets and putting up new ones became too troublesome. So Goscha had an idea—a type of paint that would turn a wall into a giant markerboard.

Most people have their own way of organizing notes and sketches of ideas.

34

By 2013, John Goscha's IdeaPaint was available in more than 50 countries.

Goscha spent the next six years working on his idea, devoting huge amounts of time, energy, and money. Many people told him it couldn't be done, but he never gave up. In 2008, he presented his finished product—IdeaPaint—at a trade show in Chicago, Illinois. It was a big success. Today, IdeaPaint is used all over the world. Goscha continues to work on new ideas, taking whatever risks are needed to turn them into reality.

Failing Is *Not* the End of the World

One of the main reasons that many people do not succeed in business is because they're afraid to fail. Let's face it, no one likes to fail. Failing can be very costly—you lose time, money, and faith in yourself. And yet no successful American entrepreneur can honestly say he or she never failed. Perhaps some idea didn't work. But the person learned something from that failure and didn't make the same mistakes next time.

Timeline of Changes in American Business

1913

Automotive entrepreneur Henry Ford starts using an assembly line in his factories, changing the way many American products are made.

1958

The first credit cards are issued in the United States, changing the way consumers buy just about everything.

Sam Walton tried all sorts of ideas to bring customers into his retail store. He advertised a low price for one item to encourage customers to come and, hopefully, buy several items. He gave away hot drinks on cold days. He also put bright, colorful items in his front window to draw people's attention. Some ideas worked. Others did not. Walton learned from every failure. And you might have heard of his retail **chain**, Walmart.

1981
The small software company Microsoft designs its first computer operating system, making it easier for people to use computers.

2004
Mark Zuckerberg launches the Facebook Web site, changing social networking and online business.

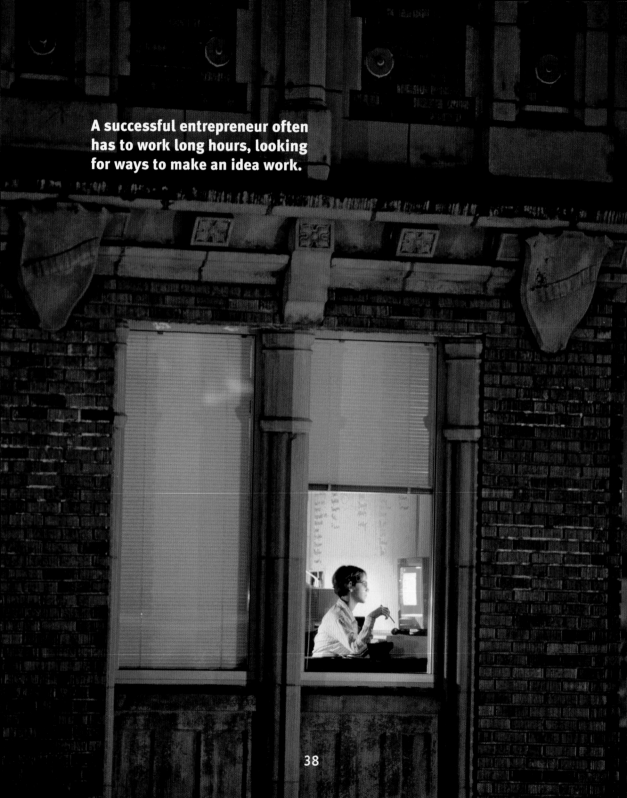

A successful entrepreneur often has to work long hours, looking for ways to make an idea work.

CHAPTER 5

The Never-Quit Attitude

If there is one quality that seems common to all successful American entrepreneurs, it's the ability to stay focused. They think constantly about what they're trying to do. They go to sleep thinking about their goals, wake up thinking about them, and sometimes even dream about them.

 A new business owner works an average of 70 hours a week.

Keeping an Eye on the Prize

Most people have heard of Bill Gates. Even if you haven't, there's a good chance you've used one of his products. He is the man who gave the world the Windows computer operating system. Gates started Microsoft—the company that makes Windows—with a friend back in the 1970s. From that day forward, he worked hard to make that company a success.

Bill Gates and Microsoft have become known for Windows, Word, Excel, PowerPoint, and other computer programs.

Gates's work ethic helped provide Microsoft with a strong start.

Gates got up early, stayed in his office late, and worked during the weekends. Even when he wasn't at work, he was *thinking* about how to improve Microsoft's products. He sometimes didn't sleep or change his clothes for days at a time. But you have to give him credit. Microsoft became one of the most successful companies ever, Gates became one of the wealthiest men on earth, and Windows forever changed the way people use computers.

A new business might experience a lot of failures before becoming successful.

Hanging Tough

Success might be fun, but it is rarely easy. Sometimes even the most brilliant businessperson gets discouraged. Someone can have an idea that other people say is no good. But a person must keep trying, even when it feels like the whole world is against the idea. This is determination, and it keeps the successful and soon-to-be successful entrepreneurs going.

Once Upon a Time

A young man named George had an idea for a great movie. George brought his idea to every studio in Hollywood, but they all told him it was no good. George kept trying. Even when he found someone to fund his movie, many people still thought George would fail. He made his movie anyway. "George" was George Lucas. The movie was *Star Wars*. It went on to become one of the most successful movies in Hollywood history. ★

Number of billionaires in the United States: More than 400

Number of millionaires in the United States: More than 3 million

America's gross domestic product (value of all goods and services produced) in 2012: More than $15 trillion

Net worth of America's wealthiest entrepreneur: Bill Gates, $66 billion

Name and worth of the three biggest companies in the United States in 2012: ExxonMobil (more than $450 billion), Walmart (more than $440 billion), and Chevron (more than $240 billion)

Number of small businesses (under 500 employees) in the United States in 2012: More than 5.5 million

Did you find the truth?

F Warren Buffett made his fortune in the computer industry.

T Andrew Carnegie made his fortune in the steel industry.

Resources

Books

Burgan, Michael. *American Capitalism*. New York: Scholastic, 2013.

Yomtov, Nel. *Starting Your Own Business*. New York: Scholastic, 2014.

Important Words

chain (CHAYN) — a group of stores that is owned by the same company and sells similar products

contracts (KAHN-trakts) — legal agreements between people or companies stating what each of them has agreed to do and any amounts of money involved

entrepreneurs (ahn-truh-pruh-NURZ) — people who start businesses and find new ways to make money

industry (IN-duh-stree) — manufacturing companies and other businesses, taken together

intuition (in-too-ISH-uhn) — an understanding of something that is based on feelings rather than reason or logic

manufacturers (man-yuh-FAK-chur-urz) — companies that make products

retailers (REE-tay-lurz) — people who sell goods to the public, usually in a store

unique (yoo-NEEK) — being the only one of its kind

ventures (VEN-churz) — risky or daring projects

visionaries (VIZH-uh-ner-eez) — people who are able to think ahead and plan

Index

Page numbers in **bold** indicate illustrations

About the Author

Wil Mara is the award-winning author of more than 140 books, many of which are educational titles for young readers.